ALTO SAXOPHONE / TENOR SAXOPHONE

Jazz
ROCK
and
R&B

CURNOW®
MUSIC

EXCLUSIVELY DISTRIBUTED BY

HAL•LEONARD®
CORPORATION

7777 W. BLUEMOUND RD. P.O. BOX 13819 MILWAUKEE, WI 53213

CD number: 19.058-3 CMP

The Artists:
Chris Vadala - alto saxophone
James Hosay - keyboards, keyboard bass, trumpet
Jason Cale - electric and acoustic guitars
Ralph Copely - drums
Keith Philbrick - saxophones
Jay Larkin - trombone on Old School Reunion
Dale Eley - Bass Guitar on Cinderella Afternoon

Mastered by Bruce Cain (Digital/Analog/Digital)

Order number: CMP 1028-05-400

Jazz Rock and R&B
James Hosay
saxophone

ISBN: 978-90-431-2271-9

James Hosay

James L. Hosay was born in Nashville, Tennessee, and raised in Norfolk, Virginia. After high school, he joined the United States Army as a trumpet player and graduated from the U.S. Armed Forces School of Music. After his first three year enlistment, he landed a job as Music Copyist for the United States Army Band (Pershing's Own) in Washington, D.C. Having aspirations of becoming a professional composer and arranger, he used this time to develop his writing skills, and in 1981 he earned the position of Staff Arranger for the United States Army Band. During his tenure as Staff Arranger, James Hosay wrote arrangements for many well-known recording artists, including Patti LaBelle, Amy Grant, Reba McEntire, and Lee Greenwood. Quite often, his music was performed for U.S. and foreign dignitaries, foreign heads of State, and the President of the United States. He was called upon to write original music for numerous high-level events, such as the re-dedication ceremonies for the Washington Monument and the U.S. Capitol Building, and most recently for the ceremony celebrating the 50th Anniversary of NATO, which was attended by the heads of State of all NATO countries.

During his 20-year military career, James Hosay received two Meritorious Service Medals, two Army Commendation Medals, and a personal letter of commendation from the Chairman of the Joint Chiefs of Staff – General Colin Powell, after writing a special march for the General's retirement ceremony. Now retired from the United States Army, James Hosay once again resides in his hometown of Norfolk, Virginia, and is an exclusive writer for CURNOW MUSIC PRESS.

Introduction

This Play-Along CD is the follow-up to JAZZ-ROCK IN THE USA, but it has blossomed into a project that explores newer territory in Jazz-Rock, Fusion, R&B, and Hip-Hop styles. Joining me in the writing duties for this project is singer, songwriter, and guitarist Jason Cale, who contributes two outstanding original tunes. The first of these is FEELIN' IT, a bright, funky fusion offering that starts things off on a positive note.

CHILLVILLE is a mellow, relaxing vacation for the mind and spirit with some rhythmic challenges for the soloist. Then you'll be ready for BOOMIN' BALLAD - a pretty R&B ballad that will allow for some very expressive playing.

RAP RIFFS explores the sounds and grooves used in Rap accompaniments. With three hip moods, you may be tempted to break into a Rap of your own. Now it's time to get hip and KICK IT with a bouncy R&B tune that will have those stereo speakers booming. CYBERNATION is a jazzy Hip-Hop invention that is both hypnotic and funky.

Jason Cale's second contribution in the writing department - J...J...JAMMIN' is a hot fusion tune with a cool Hip-Hop groove provided by drummer Ralph Copley. OLD SCHOOL REUNION takes us back to the soulful sounds of the 60s and 70s. The accompaniment track features a real horn section and some incredible guitar work by Jason Cale.

A very special woman in my life - Laura Kelly was the inspiration for CINDERELLA AFTERNOON. I must also give her credit for coming up with the title. Chris Vadala, who I had the pleasure of working with once again, provides a beautiful and tremendously expressive rendering of the solo part on the demo track.

NO END IN SIGHT can only be described as a wild musical adventure. Check out the super-hip psychedelic rock guitar licks laid down by Jason Cale on this one. Hold on and don't let go!

I hope you will enjoy playing along with these tunes as much as we enjoyed writing and producing them for you. Thanks for buying this product and good luck as you strive to reach your musical goals.

James L. Hosay

Contents

= Play Along Version

FEELIN' IT

ALTO SAXOPHONE

JASON CALE

Track: 2 3

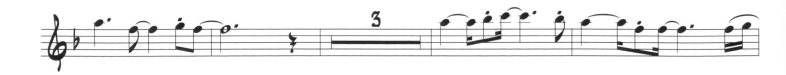

CHILLVILLE

ALTO SAXOPHONE

JAMES HOSAY

BOOMIN' BALLAD

ALTO SAXOPHONE

JAMES HOSAY

Track: 6 7

RAP RIFFS

ALTO SAXOPHONE

JAMES HOSAY

Track: 8 9

KICK IT!

ALTO SAXOPHONE

JAMES HOSAY

Copyright © 2005 by **Curnow Music Press, Inc.**

CYBER-NATION

ALTO SAXOPHONE

JAMES HOSAY

J... J... Jammin'

ALTO SAXOPHONE

JASON CALE

Funky Fusion (Swing Eigth notes)

OLD SCHOOL REUNION

ALTO SAXOPHONE

JAMES HOSAY

Track: 16 17

CINDERELLA AFTERNOON

ALTO SAXOPHONE

JAMES HOSAY

Track: 18 19

NO END IN SIGHT

ALTO SAXOPHONE

JAMES HOSAY

Track: 20 21

Jazz ROCK and R&B

FEELIN' IT

TENOR SAXOPHONE

JASON CALE

Track: 2 3

FUNKY JAZZ-ROCK

CHILLVILLE

TENOR SAXOPHONE

JAMES HOSAY

Track: 4 5

BOOMIN' BALLAD

JAMES HOSAY

Track: 6 7

SLOW R&B

RAP RIFFS

TENOR SAXOPHONE

KICK IT!

TENOR SAXOPHONE

JAMES HOSAY

Track: 10 11

CYBER-NATION

TENOR SAXOPHONE

JAMES HOSAY

J... J... JAMMIN'

TENOR SAXOPHONE

JASON CALE

Track: 14 15

Funky Fusion (Swing Eigth notes)

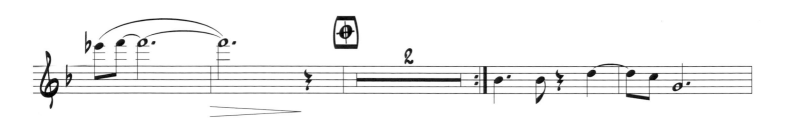

D.S. AL CODA

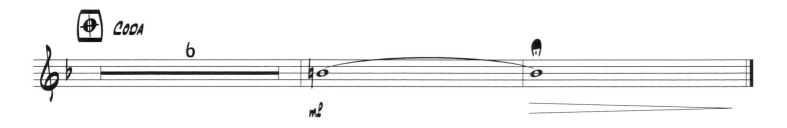

OLD SCHOOL REUNION

TENOR SAXOPHONE

JAMES HOSAY

Track: 16 17

CINDERELLA AFTERNOON

TENOR SAXOPHONE

JAMES HOSAY

Copyright © 2005 by **Curnow Music Press, Inc.**

NO END IN SIGHT

TENOR SAXOPHONE

JAMES HOSAY

Track: 20 21

Copyright © 2005 by **Curnow Music Press, Inc.**

JAZZ ROCK IN THE USA

Jazz Rock was born in the USA in the late 1960's. With it's roots solidly in R&B and rock, it ventured boldly into the harmonic complexities of jazz. Since then it has been used by pop musicians throughout the world. This book contains eight pieces in a variety of pop styles from hip-hop to blues. The play-along CD allows you to perform the pieces with your own live pop group.

Flute	CMP 0369-00-400
Clarinet	CMP 0370-00-400
Alto/Tenor Saxophone	CMP 0371-00-400
Trumpet	CMP 0373-00-400
Trombone	CMP 0374-00-400

James L. Hosay

FUN WITH FOLK AND ALTERNATIVE ROCK

Hey! Looking for something alternative? Then let's rock! There's a little bit of everything in this collection of original tunes, ranging from more traditional folk ballads, to folk rock, to alternative. Even a touch of "folk-funk" is in the mix! So kick back, sharpen your playing skills and have some fun playing along with folk rock, alternative rock and then some!

Flute	CMP 0959-00-400
Clarinet	CMP 0960-00-400
Alto Saxophone	CMP 0961-00-400
Trumpet	CMP 0962-00-400
Trombone	CMP 0963-00-400

John Hosay